To Leo and Frankie

PRELUDE

I

GERSHWIN-HEIFETZ*

*When performing this composition in public the names of the composer and transcriber must be mentioned jointly on the program. THE PUBLISHER.

PRELUDES
By
EORGE GERSHWIN
Violin and Piano

Harbor Island, Calif.
Sept. 24, 1940

PRELUDE

II

GERSHWIN-HEIFETZ*

* When performing this composition in public the names of the composer and transcriber must be mentioned jointly on the program. THE PUBLISHER.

Violin

To Leo and Frankie

PRELUDE
I

GERSHWIN-HEIFETZ*

Allegro ben ritmato e deciso (♩ = 100)

*When performing this composition in public the names of the composer and transcriber must be mentioned jointly on the program. THE PUBLISHER.

PRELUDE

Violin

II

GERSHWIN-HEIFETZ *

Andante con moto e poco rubato ($\quad$ = 88)

Tempo I

* When performing this composition in public the names of the composer and transcriber must be mentioned jointly on the program. THE PUBLISHER.

Harbor Island, Calif.
Sept. 25, 1940

PRELUDE

III

Violin

GERSHWIN-HEIFETZ*

Allegro ben ritmato e deciso (♩ = 116)

Harbor Island, Calif.
July 8, 1942

Tempo I

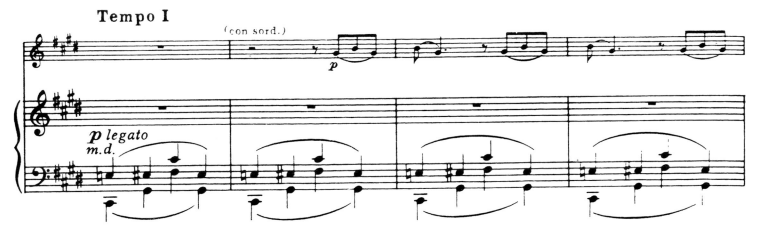

Harbor Island, Calif.
Sept. 25, 1940

PRELUDE

III

GERSHWIN-HEIFETZ*

* When performing this composition in public the names of the composer and transcriber must be mentioned jointly on the program. THE PUBLISHER.

Harbor Island, Calif
July 8, 1942